MY KOREAN ALPHABET COLORING BOOK

THIS BOOK BELONGS TO:

Learn the Korean Vowels, Numbers, and Colors !

MIGHTYFORTRESS
PRESS

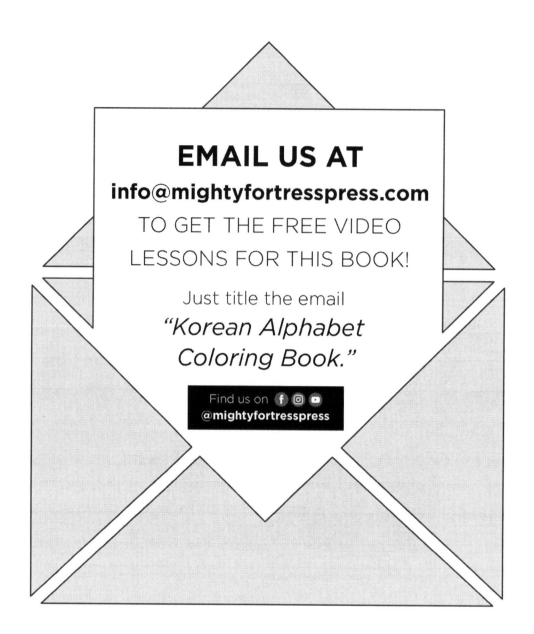

EMAIL US AT
info@mightyfortresspress.com
TO GET THE FREE VIDEO
LESSONS FOR THIS BOOK!

Just title the email
"Korean Alphabet
Coloring Book."

Find us on
@mightyfortresspress

ISBN NO: 978-1-7328644-2-9
Text and illustrations Copyright 2020 by Mighty Fortress Press.

For general information on our other products, please contact our Customer Care Department within the U.S. by going to our website at www.mightyfortresspress.com.

Kang, Eunice, author.
Koh, Young Jae, book designer.
"Magic Hangul Collection"

TABLE
OF
CONTENTS

NOTE TO PARENTS

Welcome to *My Korean Alphabet Coloring Book of Vowels!* As an educator and a parent, I made this book because I wanted to teach my children the basics of Korean with instructions in the English language. To get the most out of this book, please take your time going through each page together with your child and practice how to say the sounds and names for each letter and word.

The illustrations are paired with the words written in Korean and in English phonetically so that Korean as second language learners can pronounce the Korean words. And even though this book is primarily a coloring book for young children, it could also be used as flashcards for older kids and beginner adults.

This book is divided into 4 units:
- 10 basic vowels
- Numbers 1-10 in native Korean *(Hangul)*
- Numbers 1-10 in Sino-Korean *(Hanja)*
- 13 colors

There is a plethora of research that suggests learning a second language can boost the brain! Learning a second language benefits not only children as they learn to speak but also adults as they age. I hope that you and your family will find this book useful with hours of fun, coloring, and lots of learning. Thank you again for choosing this book.

Happy coloring and learning!

-Eunice Kang, Ph.D.

UNIT 1

VOWELS

[mo-eum]

Note: In this unit, we will learn 10 basic vowels. The "O" consonant is a placeholder to show where each consonant goes next to each vowel.

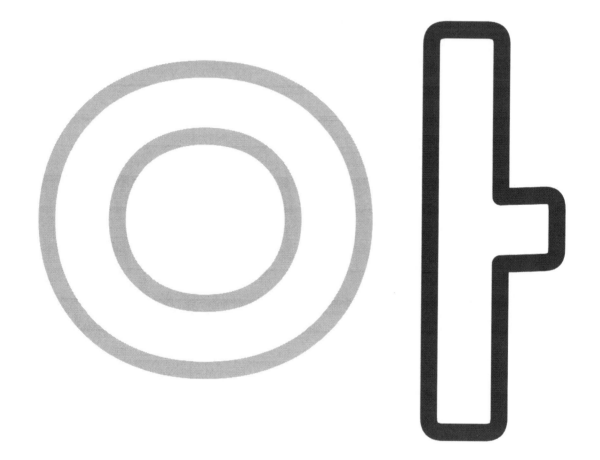

[ah]

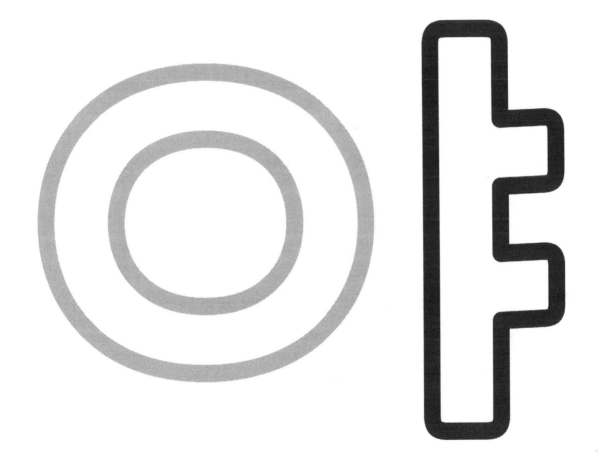

[ya]

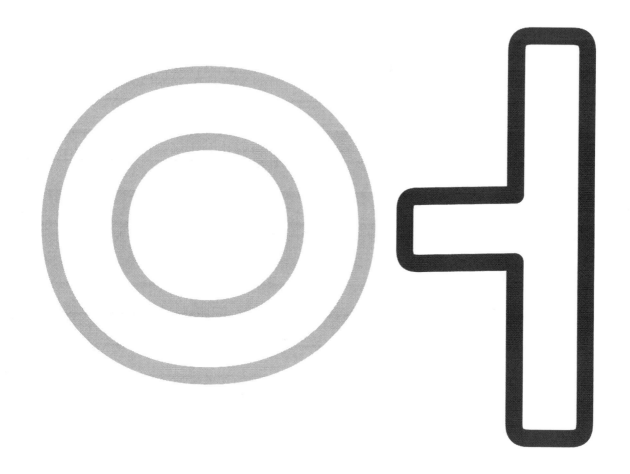

[uh]

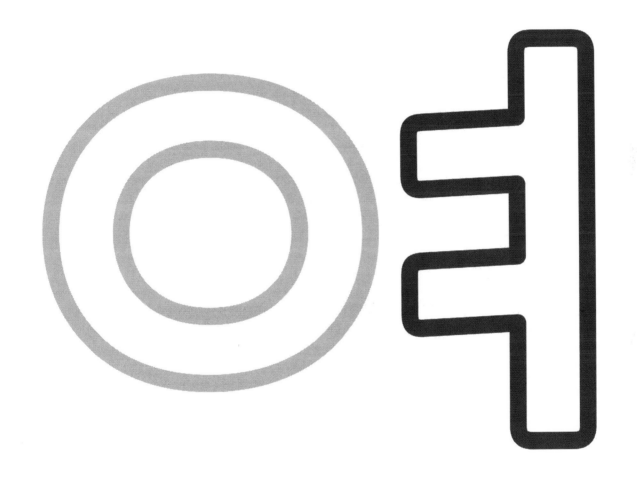

[yuh]

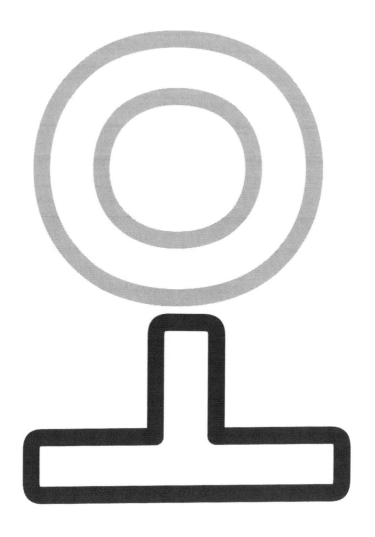

[oh]

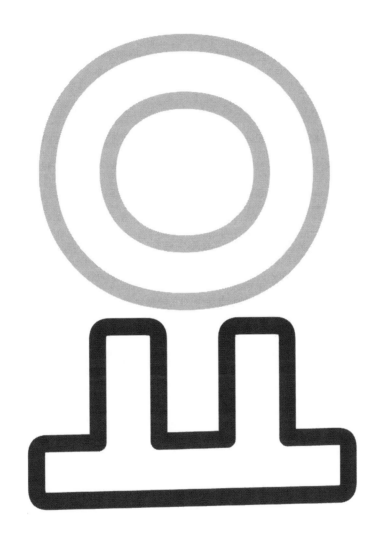

[yo]

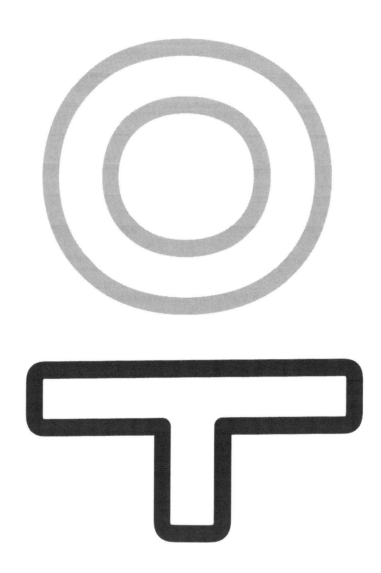

[oo]

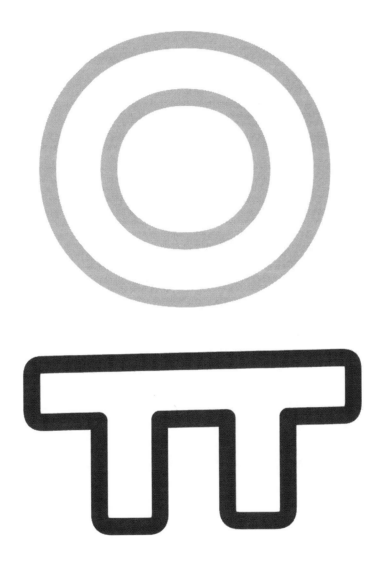

[yoo]

[euh]

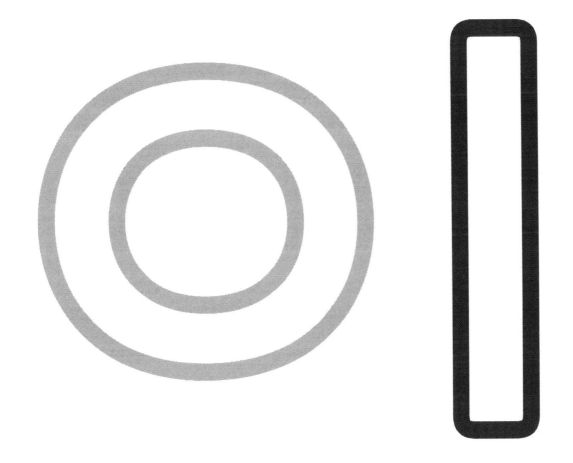

[ee]

Recap of Unit 1
Vowels
모음 [mo-eum]

I. Vowels with "ㅇ" placeholder

아	야	어	여
[ah]	[ya]	[uh]	[yuh]
오	요	우	유
[oh]	[yo]	[oo]	[yoo]
		으	이
		[euh]	[ee]

II. Vowels by itself

ㅏ	ㅑ	ㅓ	ㅕ
[ah]	[ya]	[uh]	[yuh]
ㅗ	ㅛ	ㅜ	ㅠ
[oh]	[yo]	[oo]	[yoo]
		ㅡ	ㅣ
		[euh]	[ee]

UNIT 2

NUMBERS

[soot-ja]

Note: In this unit, we will learn the numbers (1-10) in native Korean (Hangul).

하나

[hana]

2

둘

[dul]

셋

[set]

넷

[net]

다섯

[da-seot]

여섯

[yeo-seot]

[il-gop]

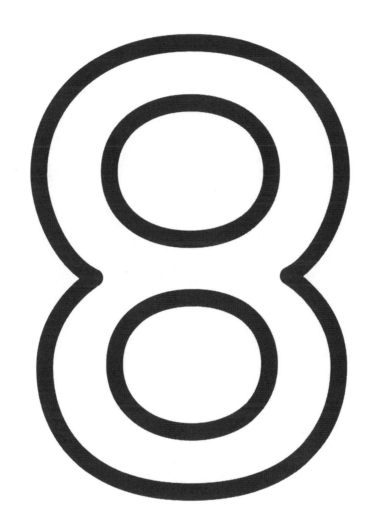

여덟

[yeo-deol]

[ah-hope]

10

열

[yeol]

Recap of Unit 2
Numbers in Native Korean
한글

I. Numbers in native Korean (한글)

1	2	3	4	5
하나	둘	셋	넷	다섯
[hana]	[dul]	[set]	[net]	[da-seot]

6	7	8	9	10
여섯	일곱	여덟	아홉	열
[yeo-seot]	[il-gop]	[yeo-deol]	[ah-hope]	[yeol]

UNIT 3

NUMBERS

숫자

[soot-ja]

Note: In this unit, we will learn the numbers (1-10) in Sino-Korean (Hanja).

[il]

이

[ee]

[sahm]

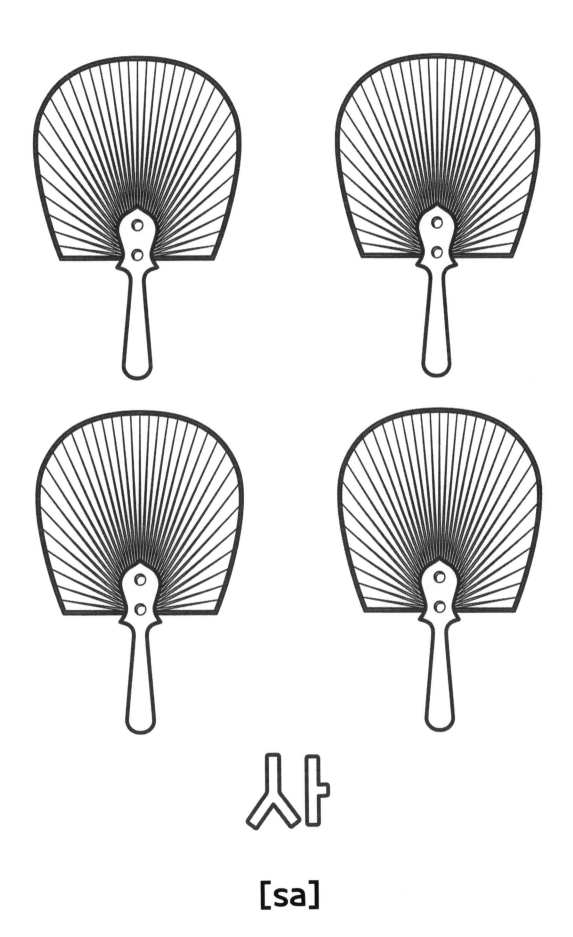

사

[sa]

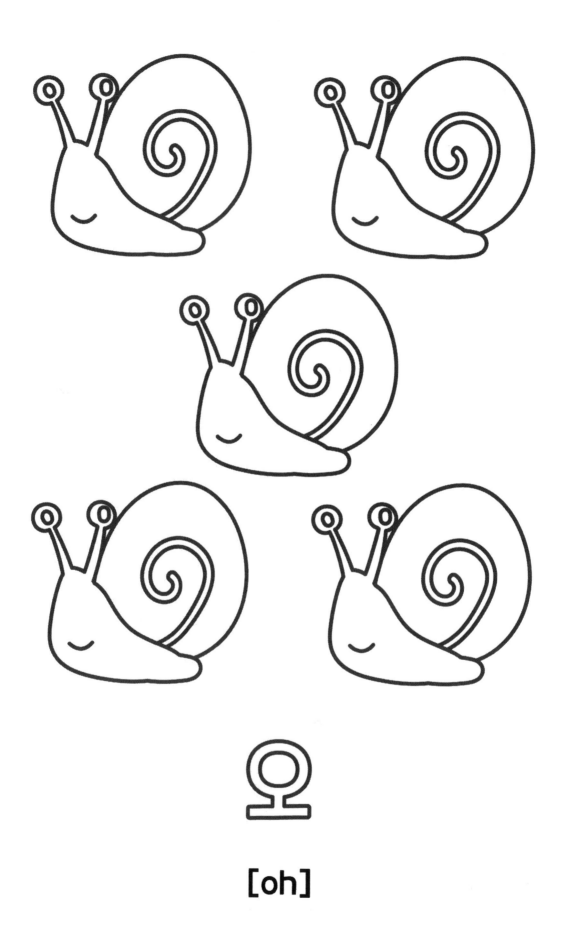

오

[oh]

육

[yook]

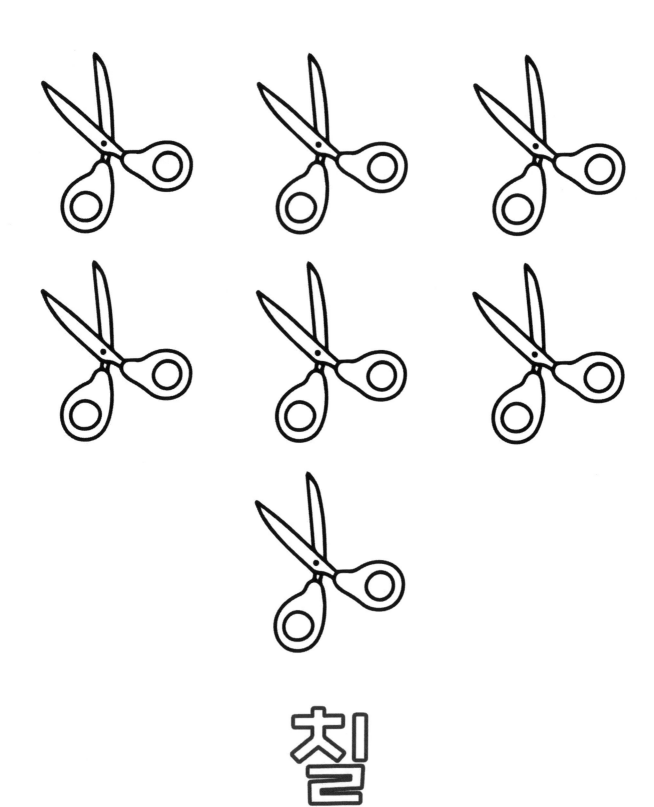

칠

[chil]

[pal]

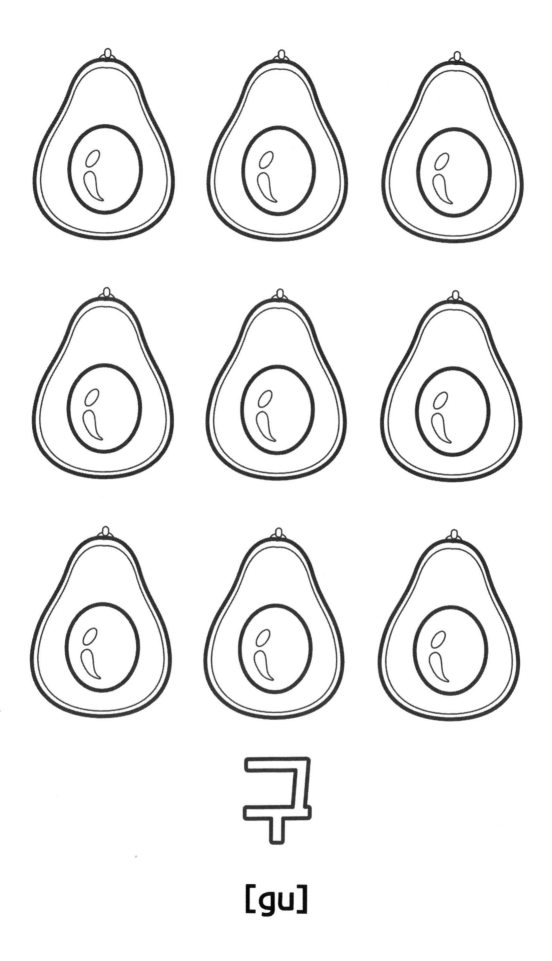

[gu]

[ship]

Recap of Unit 3
Numbers in Sino-Korean (Hanja)
한자

II. Numbers in Sino-Korean (한자)

1	2	3	4	5
일	이	삼	사	오
[il]	[ee]	[sahm]	[sa]	[oh]

6	7	8	9	10
육	칠	팔	구	십
[yook]	[chil]	[pal]	[gu]	[ship]

UNIT 4

COLORS

[sek-kkal]

Note: In this unit, we will learn 13 different colors.

[bbal-gan-sek]

[ju-hwang-sek]

[no-ran-sek]

초록색

[cho-rok-sek]

[pa-ran-sek]

보라색

[bo-ra-sek]

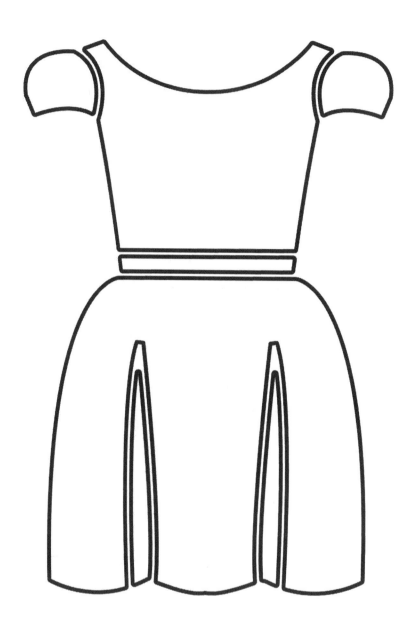

[boon-hong-sek]

[gkal-sek]

[kka-man-sek]

하얀색

[ha-yan-sek]

회색

[hweh-sek]

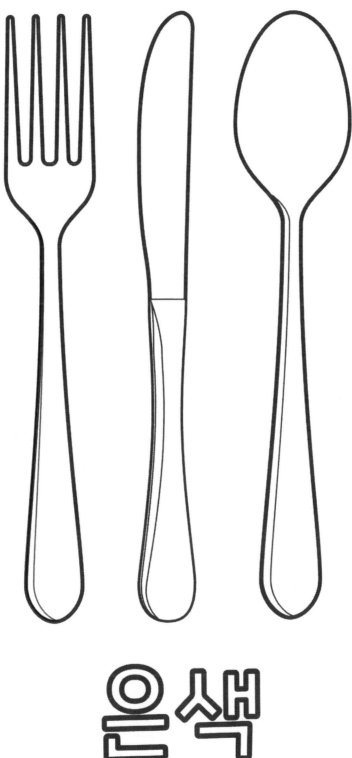

은색

[eun-sek]

금색

[geum-sek]

Recap of Unit 4
Colors

색깔 [sek-kkal]

빨간색	주황색	노란색	초록색	파란색
[bbal-gan-sek]	[ju-hwang-sek]	[no-ran-sek]	[cho-rok-sek]	[pa-ran-sek]

보라색	분홍색	갈색	까만색	하얀색
[bo-ra-sek]	[boon-hong-sek]	[gkal-sek]	[kka-man-sek]	[ha-yan-sek]

회색	은색	금색
[hweh-sek]	[eun-sek]	[geum-sek]

Rainbow

무지개 [moo-ji-gae]

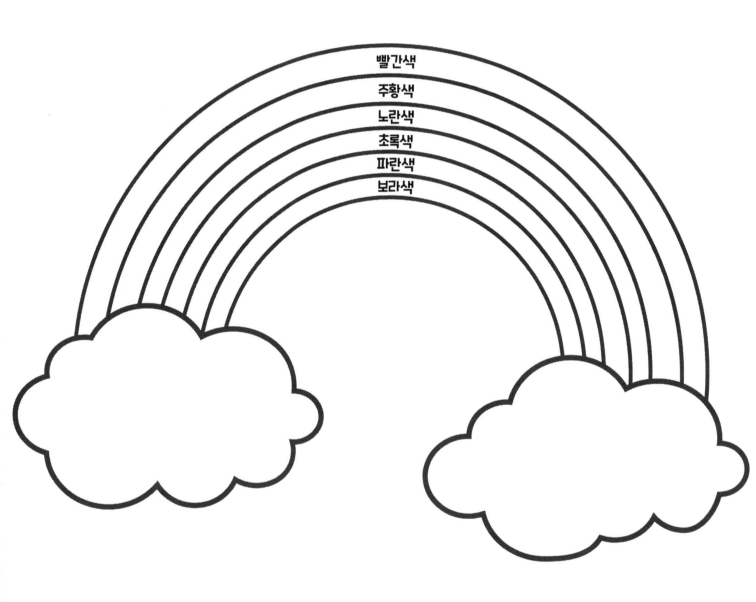

빨간색
주황색
노란색
초록색
파란색
보라색

Author

Eunice Kang, Ph.D. is an educator in Los Angeles, California. Her research areas include South Korea and Korean language policy. She loved coloring as a child and now loves coloring with her own two children.

 @eunicekangbooks

Book Designer

Young Jae Koh is a graphic designer based in Los Angeles, California. She has previously worked in Korea and New York as an art director. She loves to watercolor and create art with her daughter.

 @youngjaekoh

CHECK OUT MORE BOOKS BY MIGHTY FORTRESS PRESS!

Korean Writing Book

Coming Soon.

Made in the USA
Middletown, DE
21 August 2020